Contents

Introduction

Welcome to REVELATION: UNLOCKING THE MYSTERIES WITH YOUTH! This experience recaptures the hopeful message of the Book of Revelation. In the common "gloom and doom" interpretations of the Book of Revelation, the emphasis is upon everything disturbing and frightening about the last book of the Bible. This study, however, reminds us that Revelation was not meant to be a "blueprint for the end of the world." Instead, Revelation was to inspire hope and courage in the hearts of first-century Christians who were persecuted for their beliefs. The Christians of John's day faced humiliation, segregation, prison, torture, and even death because they chose to follow Jesus Christ.

Through the Book of Revelation, John reminded these persecuted Christians that a loving God was in control of creation and that evil would not win in the end. Although much of Revelation is about judgment, the book shows us that no one who lives a life of faith built on God's loving grace needs to fear judgment. As 1 John says,

> *Love has been perfected among us in this: that we may have boldness on the day of judgment, because as [Jesus] is, so are we in this world. There is no fear in love, but perfect love casts out fear; for fear has to do with punishment, and whoever fears has not reached perfection in love. We love because he first loved us.* (1 John 4:17-19)

This study will take the fear out of reading Revelation and open our eyes to the true message of the Bible's most misunderstood book. Revelation proclaims that even in the darkest of times, there is reason to hope: God is always there, and God's power and goodness will always prevail over evil and God will take care of those who remain faithful.

You may begin or end this study of the Book of Revelation with an experience designed to help persons understand what it is like to be persecuted. The Catacomb Lock-In (page 33) will put youth in the mindset of the early persecuted Christians. What did those Christians face on a day-to-day basis? How did they think? What did they feel? Few people, especially in this country, understand what it means to be persecuted.

The Catacomb Lock-In will also make youth aware of the many Christians who are persecuted throughout the world today at the turn of the 21st Century. How do those Christians find hope? If you really want to know, if you're ready for hope—step into the catacomb!

EVEN IN THE DARKEST OF TIMES, THERE IS REASON TO HOPE:

God is always there!

What is The Catacomb Project?

The Catacomb Project is a major initiative to reach youth with a message of hope and a call to faithful living. Teenagers in this country may not experience severe persecution for their faith as did the first-century Christians and as do persons in other countries even today. However, for many different reasons, youth face their own dark times. To go *through* those times, they need the message of hope and the call to faithfulness, which are at the heart of the Book of Revelation. The Catacomb Project, including this study of Revelation, is one way to give to young persons the courage for living that comes from life-abundant in Jesus Christ!

THE LOCK-IN OF THE MILLENNIUM

The Catacomb Project: Hope for 2000 and Beyond (ISBN 0-687-07491-6) presents a specialized version of the Catacomb Lock-In found in this study (pages 33–43). The Lock-In is an opportunity to unite your group with youth from other churches and to share this common experience with the worldwide Christian community.

On December 31, 1999, youth will be "kidnapped and smuggled" into an as true-to-life exile experience as possible. Youth will experience a community of faith like that of the Christians in the catacombs during a time of persecution. On the next day, they will emerge with a joyous worship celebration.

The Catacomb Project: Hope for 2000 and Beyond includes specific Y2K references, instructions for linking youth groups on New Year's Eve through live Internet chat, and other ways that will make the turn of the calendar meaningful and memorable.

With the Catacomb Project, youth will usher in the New Year with the promise of a hope-filled future.

How to Use this Resource

This resource has two parts:

1. REVELATION: A STUDY USING *Unlocking the Mysteries: 150 FAQs About Revelation and the End of the World*

2. THE CATACOMB LOCK-IN: AN IMMERSION EXPERIENCE

You may use each part independently, but you'll get best results by tying them together. We recommend two options:

THE REVELATION STUDY SESSIONS AS PREPARATION FOR THE CATACOMB LOCK-IN:

1st Week	Session 1: Who, What, When, Where, Why, and How?
2nd Week	Session 2: How Soon is Soon? Or How Can Soon Not Be Soon?
3rd Week	Session 3: The Players: Good Guys, Bad Guys, Beastie Boys and Girls
4th Week	Session 4: What's Happening Here? Places and Events
5th Week	Session 5: Are These Sevens Lucky or Unlucky?
6th Week	Session 6: What Would Jesus Do, and What Would Jesus Have Us Do, About the End of the World?
Last Weekend	Catacomb Lock-In in four sessions

THE REVELATION STUDY SESSIONS AS FOLLOW-UP TO THE CATACOMB LOCK-IN:

First Weekend Catacomb Lock-In in four sessions

2nd Week   Session 1: Who, What, When, Where, Why, and How?

3rd Week   Session 2: How Soon is Soon? Or How Can Soon Not Be Soon?

4th Week   Session 3: The Players: Good Guys, Bad Guys, Beastie Boys and Girls

5th Week   Session 4: What's Happening Here? Places and Events

6th Week   Session 5: Are These Sevens Lucky or Unlucky?

Last Week   Session 6: What Would Jesus Do, and What Would Jesus Have Us Do, About the End of the World?

Use this resource in the way that best fits the personality and interests of your group. It can be used as a short-term study, a Lenten experience, a summertime adventure, or your New Year's youth tradition in the making.

Revelation

A STUDY USING

Unlocking the Mysteries:
150 FAQs About Revelation and the End of the World

Using These Sessions

The six sessions in this study are based on *Unlocking the Mysteries: 150 FAQs About Revelation and the End of the World* (Abingdon, 0-687-08708-2). For best results (and for a good read!) each youth should have a copy to use with the sessions. It is crucial that the study leader have a copy of the book.

You can use these sessions in a variety of ways:

- As a weekly study
- For a weekend retreat
- With the Catacomb Lock-in or independently
- In preparation for the Catacomb Lock-In
- As a follow up the Catacomb Lock-In

You determine what is best for your group. See "How to Use This Resource" on page 4 for further ideas.

PRIZES AND SUCH

Sessions 2, 4, 5, and 6 offer fun activities that result in a winner or winners. If you decide to award prizes to the winners, appropriate incentives could include The Catacomb Project T-shirts, caps, or jewelry. You could also offer a "last will be first" award to the youth who brings up the rear, or give all the youth who participate a Catacomb Project momento. (Check cover for ordering information.)

REVELATION TIMELINE

The Revelation timeline is the most important visual aid you will use during the course of this study. These sessions do not follow the standard Bible-study format of working chapter by chapter through the Book of Revelation. So the Revelation Timeline helps youth visualize how all of the pieces fit into the larger picture and continuity of the Book of Revelation. See pages 28–29 for an example.

To construct a large Revelation timeline for your room, you will need a long sheet (22–44 feet) of butcher paper or twenty-two large sheets of paper. Draw lines on the butcher paper to create sections, one for each of the twenty-two chapters of the Book of Revelation. Allow a foot or two of space for each chapter. On this wall chart, the youth will keep track of how each person, place, or event fits into the Book of Revelation. In each session there is time alotted for youth to draw or write something to help them keep track.

REVELATION CREATIONS

As you go through the study, make time for youth to respond expressively to the figures, events, and messages of Revelation. Invite youth to work independently or in groups to create art, montages, collages, music, poetry, or drama inspired by their study of Revelation. Some youth may choose to write their thoughts about and reactions to what they are learning about Revelation in a journal. Each session will allow time for youth to work on their creations.

THEME SONG

To close each session or while the youth are working on the timeline or their creations, play or sing a specific song. The following musical artists have recorded songs that carry the hopeful themes of Revelation. All are available on CD; most are available as sheet music or in songbooks from a Christian bookstore.

Artist	Song	Album
Kirk Franklin	"Revolution"	*The Nu Nation Project* (GospoCentric)
Third Day	"My Hope Is in You"	*Conspiracy No. 5* (Reunion)
Deliriou5?	"I Could Sing of Your Love"	*Cutting Edge* (Sparrow)
CeCe Winans	"Well, Alright"	*Everlasting Love* (PMG/ Sparrow)
Mukala	"Skip to the End"	*Fiction* (essential)
Avalon	"The Move"	*A Maze of Grace* (Sparrow)
Blues Brothers	"John the Revelator"	*Blues Brothers 2000* (Universal)
Third Day	"Agnus Dei"	*Exodus* (Rocketown)

DIFFERENT WAYS OF LEARNING

Music, reflection, creative expressions, the logic of a timeline, and discussion are all important. People have different ways of learning. Use as many as you can in this encounter with the Book of Revelation.

Who, What, When, Where, Why, and How?

Focus:

The Christians of John's time were persecuted, imprisoned, and even put to death for believing in Jesus Christ. John felt his vision would give them courage and hope to face the future, resting in the knowledge that a good and loving God was ultimately in control.

Focus Scripture:

Blessed is the one who reads aloud the words of the prophecy, and blessed are those who hear and who keep what is written in it; for the time is near.

Revelation 1:3

Additional Scriptures:

Any or all of the first chapter of the Book of Revelation

Materials:

† stuff for Revelation timeline. See page 7.
† index cards
† pens or pencils
† items for individual and group creations. See page 7.

Before the Session:

Gather materials. Make all necessary preparations for the Revelation timeline to be in place.

KEY POINTS

† Scholars disagree about whether the John who wrote the Book of Revelation is the same John who wrote the Gospel of John (the "Beloved Disciple").

† The John who wrote the Book of Revelation may have had a leadership role in the church in Asia Minor where the seven churches referred to in Revelation are located. John was exiled to the island of Patmos for witnessing and preaching in the name of Jesus Christ.

† The Book of Revelation was most likely written between A.D. 90 and 100 during a time of persecution.

† Prophecy is God's appropriate word to God's people in a particular time and place—not a prediction of future events.

† The Book of Revelation has two important messages:

1. In the end God's loving goodness will prevail over all evil, and God will take care of those who remain faithful.

2. Christians are to live out their faith in acts of love and service.

THE REVEALER
(10 minutes)

As youth arrive, give each person an index card and a pen or pencil. Have the youth sit on the floor in a circle and write down a fact about themselves that nobody else in the group knows. The fact may be a personality trait, a childhood memory, a school grade, or an identification number.

Collect the cards and shuffle them. Read one card aloud. The group will try to determine who wrote the fact.

The person who wrote the fact will attempt to wink at each of the other members of the group. When a person is winked at, she should say "It's not me" and put her head down.

The other players can guess the name of the revealer. If the guess is incorrect, the guesser must put his head down. If the guess is correct, award a prize and read the next card.

Play at least three rounds. Then **SAY**:

Most of us hold back something about ourselves that nobody else knows. As we get closer to people, we reveal more of those secrets. The Book of Revelation is about the revealing of secrets. As we get to know it better, we will understand its purpose and messages; but some questions will remain hidden, including details like "Who exactly is John, the Revealer?"

Q AND A
(20–30 minutes)

The question-and-answer format of the FAQ book, *Unlocking the Mysteries*, gives you a natural flow to follow in exploring the background issues surrounding the Book of Revelation. You will have richer discussion if participants have read the section to be discussed and already have questions in mind when they come to Bible study.

Have youth gather in three teams. Be sure each group has at least one Bible and a copy of *Unlocking the Mysteries*.

† **WHAT DO YOU
THINK OF THESE
ANSWERS?**
† **HOW DO THESE
ANSWERS MAKE
YOU FEEL?**

Choose questions from Chapter 1 or use the selected questions below. Award three points to the first team to get the correct answer. For added suspense make your final question worth twelve points. Refer to the FAQ indicated from *Unlocking the Mysteries* for the answers. Tally the points and congratulate the winners.

Encourage the youth to discuss the FAQs that raise questions for them.

† Who was John the Revealer? (FAQ 1, 2, 3)

† Where was the Book of Revelation written? (FAQ 4, 5)

† When was the Book of Revelation written? (FAQ 7)

† Why so many weird creatures, symbols, people, and places? (FAQ 9)

† What is prophecy? (FAQ 8, 17, 18, 19)

† Why is it important to discuss the Book of Revelation today? (FAQ 28, 29)

† Do I have to believe "one way" about the Book of Revelation in order to be a Christian? (FAQ 30)

 *Key Question*

What do these answers mean for how we live as Christians?

TIMELINE AND CREATIONS
(15–45 minutes)

Introduce youth to the Revelation timeline. **SAY:**

> During every session, we will have a chance to add to our timeline of Revelation. This timeline has one section for each chapter of the Book of Revelation. You'll have a chance to draw pictures or write your impressions on the timeline. You may also work alone or with friends to create collages, montages, sculptures, songs, poems, or skits based on what we learn. We'll call them "Revelation Creations."

Allow time for participants to begin the timeline and their creations.

CLOSING
(Optional)

If you are studying in successive days or weeks, close each day by reciting the greeting from Revelation 1:4. To teach it, have a leader line it out a phrase at a time for the rest of the youth to repeat.

> *Grace to you and peace from God who is and who was and who is to come…and from Jesus Christ.*

Send the group away with a theme song. (See introduction, page 7.)

How Soon Is Soon?
OR HOW CAN SOON NOT BE SOON?

Focus:
What does the Book of Revelation mean when it uses the word *soon* for the events it describes?

Focus Scripture:
The revelation of Jesus Christ, which God gave him to show his servants what must soon take place; he made it known by sending his angel to his servant John, who testified to the word of God and to the testimony of Jesus Christ, even to all that he saw.

Revelation 1:1-2

Additional Scriptures:
Revelation 22:6-21

Materials:
† materials for the Revelation timeline
† materials for Revelation Creations
† timer
† paper for "scrolls"
† sealing wax and seal, or either stickers or stamps and envelopes (Seals and seal presses can be purchased at most card and stationery shops.)

Before the Session:
Gather materials. Make sure the Revelation timeline is posted.

KEY POINTS:

† John tells us in Revelation 1:1-3 and Revelation 22:6-21, the so-called "bookends" of Revelation, that what he is describing will happen "soon." He uses phrases like:

- "things which must soon take place" (1:1);
- "for the time is near" (1:3);
- "must soon take place" (22:6);
- "behold, I come quickly" (22:7);
- "for the time is at hand" (22:10);
- "behold, I am coming quickly" (22:12);
- "surely, I come quickly" (22:20).

✝ Either what is described in the Book of Revelation is still to take place in the future, or God decided not to bring an end to creation as described in John's vision.

How Soon Is Soon?
(10–15 minutes)

Have the youth stand with their backs against one wall. Set a timer for a random amount of time from fifteen seconds to two minutes. The youth have to judge when the timer will go off. Anyone who gets to the wall on the other side of the room before the timer goes off is "safe." Anyone who is left at the back wall when the timer goes off is "left behind." The last person to move from the "left behind wall" to the "safe wall" before the timer buzzes is the winner. Play several rounds if your group is enjoying the game.

Q & A
(20–30 minutes)

Chapter 2 of *Unlocking the Mysteries: 150 FAQs about Revelation and the End of the World* should generate lively discussion, especially around the question of whether God's mind can change. As usual, the best discussions will come if the youth have read the section and already have questions in mind when they arrive.

SAY:

As in the opening game, waiting is easier if we know how long we will have to wait and if we know the outcome of the wait. In the Book of Revelation, John talks of events that will happen soon, but we're not sure how soon soon is.

Have youth form three teams. Be sure each group has at least one Bible and a copy of *Unlocking the Mysteries*. Ask aloud each question from Chapter 2 or use the selected questions listed below. Award three points for the first team to get the correct answer. For added suspense make your final question worth twelve points. Refer to the FAQ indicated from *Unocking the Mysteries* for the answers. Tally the points and congratulate the winners.

Encourage the youth to discuss the FAQs that interest them.

✝ Does John tell us that the events he is describing are going to happen soon? (FAQ 33)

✝ What does it mean when Revelation says "soon" and "near at hand" ? (FAQ 34)

✝ How does not sealing up a scroll fit into what John means when he says "soon"? (FAQ 35)

To Further Stimulate Discussion, Also Use These Questions:

✝ **What do you think of these answers?**

✝ **How do these answers make you feel?**

† Can God's timing be different from human timing? (FAQ 37)

† Why didn't the stuff John describes happen soon? (FAQ 40, 41)

† Will God end the world the way God told John the world would end almost 2,000 years ago? (FAQ 42)

 *Key Question*

What do these answers mean for how we live as Christians?

SEAL A SCROLL
(10 minutes)

Give each person a sheet of paper for a scroll. Have the youth attempt to predict something that will happen in their personal lives, in their school or youth group, or in world events before your Revelation study. Have them write the prediction on the scroll. Then they can roll their paper into a scroll and seal it with wax; or fold it and put it in an envelope, sealing the scroll with wax or an adhesive sticker or stamp. Save the predictions for Session 5. At that time, open the scrolls and award a prize to anyone whose prediction came true.

TIMELINE AND CREATIONS
(15–45 minutes)

Direct youth to the Revelation timeline and have them fill it in for Chapters 1 and 22. Invite them to draw or write relevant material on the timeline.

Encourage those who have begun Revelation creations (sculptures, paintings, songs, poems, skits, or journals) to continue their work.

CLOSING
(Optional)

Close by reciting the greeting from Revelation 1:4:

> *Grace to you and peace from God who is and who was and who is to come…and from Jesus Christ.*

Send the group away with a theme song. (See introduction, page 7.)

Focus:

Apocalyptic writings use strange images. These images are intended to be symbolic.

Focus Scripture:

Then I turned to see whose voice it was that spoke to me, and on turning I saw seven golden lampstands, and in the midst of the lampstands I saw one like the Son of Man, clothed with a long robe and with a golden sash across his chest. His head and his hair were white as white wool, white as snow; his eyes were like a flame of fire, his feet were like burnished bronze, refined as in a furnace, and his voice was like the sound of many waters. In his right hand he held seven stars, and from his mouth came a sharp, two-edged sword, and his face was like the sun shining with full force. When I saw him, I fell at his feet as though dead. But he placed his right hand on me, saying, "Do not be afraid; I am the first and the last, and the living one. I was dead, and see, I am alive forever and ever; and I have the keys of Death and of Hades.   Revelation 1:12-18

Additional Scriptures:

Any of the pasages listed next to any of the FAQs in this section of *Unlocking the Mysteries*.

Materials:

† materials for the Revelation timeline
† paper and markers
† names of historical figures who have been accused of being the antichrist
† straight pins, safety pins, or tape

Before the Session:

Gather materials. Write each of the following names for "Who's the antichrist?" on its own sheet of paper:

Roman Emperor Nero	Adolph Hitler	Pope John Paul II
Bill Clinton	Mikhail Gorbachev	Keanu Reeves
Prince Charles of Wales	Marilyn Manson	John F. Kennedy
Barney, the Dinosaur	Napoleon	Saddam Hussein
Louis Farrakhan	Sam Donaldson	Sun Myung Moon
Roman Catholic Church	David Hasselhoff	Ronald Reagan
Bill Gates	Henry Kissinger	Pope Paul VI
Benito Mussolini	Josef Stalin	

KEY POINTS

† Images such as the Son of Man, the Lamb, and the lone rider on the white horse are meant to show us that God and the power of good will always prevail over the power of evil.

† The word *antichrist* is never mentioned in the Book of Revelation. In 1 and 2 John "antichrist" refers to a capacity to deny Christ and failure to demonstrate Christlike behavior. Given this understanding, *any* person can be "anti-Christ."

† The number 666 can be shown to be a symbolic representation of Nero.

WHO'S THE ANTICHRIST?
(10–15 minutes)

Pin a name from the "antichrist list" (page 15) on the back of each participant. Do not let the participants see their own names.

SAY:

On your back is the name of someone who has been identified as the antichrist. To find out the name on your back, you may walk around and ask yes or no questions.

Play for ten minutes, or until all participants have guessed their names. Then **SAY:**

Throughout history many people have been identified as the antichrist. But the Bible speaks about the antichrist in a different way. Let's look at some questions to understand better.

Q & A
(20–30 minutes)

Youth will undoubtedly have read or heard interpretations of Revelation that align these images with current and future events, persons, and nations. Allow the youth to discuss freely and use their imaginations, but help them see that these images are symbolic. Also emphasize that the intention of the Book of Revelation was to give hope to those being persecuted by assuring them that God was in control and that good would triumph in the end.

Have youth divide into three teams. Be sure each group has at least one Bible and a copy of *Unlocking the Mysteries*. Ask aloud any questions you choose from Chapter 3 or use the selected questions below. Award three points for the first team to get the correct answer. For added suspense make your final question worth twelve points. Refer to the FAQs indicated from *Unlocking the Mysteries* for the answers. Tally the points and congratulate the winners.

Encourage the youth to discuss the questions that especially interest them.

† Who is the Son of Man? (FAQ 46)

† Who is the lamb? (FAQ 49, 50, 51)

† Who is Satan? (FAQ 58, 59)

† Does Satan have power over us? (FAQ 60)

† Who is the beast? (FAQ 64, 65, 66, 67)

† What is the mark of the beast? (FAQ 70)

† What is the mysterious number 666? (FAQ 73, 74, 75)

† Who is the antichrist? (FAQ 78, 79)

† Where does the idea of the antichrist come from? (FAQ 80)

Key Question

What do these answers mean for how we live as Christians?

TIMELINE AND CREATIONS
(15–45 minutes)

Direct youth to the Revelation timeline and have them fill it in for Chapters 1, 2, 4, 5, 6, 7, 9, 12, 13, 14, 16, 17, 19 and 20. Invite them to draw or write relevant material on the timeline.

Allow those who have begun other creative expressions (collage, montages, sculptures, paintings, songs, poems, skits, or journals) to continue work on their creations.

CLOSING
(Optional)

Close by reciting the greeting from Revelation 1:4:

> *Grace to you and peace from God who is and who was and who is to come…and from Jesus Christ.*

Send the group away with a theme song. (See introduction, page 7.)

What's Happening Here?
PLACES AND EVENTS

Focus:

All the events of the Book of Revelation move toward the great moment when God and the human beings who have persevered in their faith are together in heaven.

Focus Scripture:

Then I saw a new heaven and a new earth; for the first heaven and the first earth had passed away, and the sea was no more. And I saw the holy city, the new Jerusalem, coming down out of heaven from God, prepared as a bride adorned for her husband. And I heard a loud voice from the throne saying, "See, the home of God is among mortals. He will dwell with them as their God; they will be his peoples, and God himself will be with them; he will wipe every tear from their eyes. Death will be no more; mourning and crying and pain will be no more, for the first things have passed away." And the one who was seated on the throne said, "See, I am making all things new."....Those who conquer will inherit these things, and I will be their God and they will be my children.

Revelation 21:1-5, 7

Additional Scriptures:

Any of the Scriptures listed next to any of the FAQs in this section of *Unlocking the Mysteries.*

Materials:

† stuff for the Revelation timeline
† index cards
† examples of 1,000
† chairs, paper, and tape for "The Number Game"

Before the Session:

Make sure you have everything prepared to continue the Revelation timeline and have gathered everything you will need for the activities you have chosen.

KEY POINTS

† The concept of the rapture results more from certain teaching traditions in the church than from what the Bible actually has to say. It has, however, been linked to Revelation in a variety of ways. One thing is clear, there is no passage in the Book of Revelation that tells us that only the faithful and true Christians will be taken out of the world.

✝ A millennium is a period of a thousand years. It is likely that the writer of the Book of Revelation was referring to the idea of "completion" rather than to a literal time period of 1,000 years.

✝ Armageddon has come to be seen as the final battle, the last great confrontation between good and evil. But the battle never takes place! God destroys the forces of evil before the battle can begin.

✝ The Book of Revelation teaches the concept of a final, ultimate judgment. With great clarity and certainty, John describes a gathering of all people who have lived for a time of judgment. There is, in John's vision, a resurrection of everyone who has died. They all stand before the Great White Throne on which God is seated and each is judged "according to the record of his or her deeds."

✝ The place where the faithful will live eternally will be the New Jerusalem, constructed by God. John tells us that God will dwell with the faithful in the New Jerusalem. This is what makes the New Jerusalem a "heavenly place." God will spend eternity with the faithful.

THE NUMBER GAME
(15 minutes)

To set up the game, have group members sit in chairs in a circle and number off beginning with number one. Have each person write the number on a sheet of paper and tape it to the inside back of the chair. Have the last person write "1000," instead of her number. The number belongs to the chair not the person. As persons move from chair to chair, their number changes.

The person seated in the chair labeled number 1 is the beginning caller. To begin the game, the caller can call out any number in the group except his or hers or one that has already been called. The person whose number is called has one second to call another number. If players make a mistake, they must go to the chair labeled number 1. All players below the caller who made the mistake move up a chair. The object is to get to the chair labeled 1000.

For example, your group has eight people, and the chairs are numbered 1, 2, 3, 4, 5, 6, 7, and 1000. The beginning caller shouts out, "Five!" The person in chair number 5 then calls out, "Seven!" but the person in chair number 7 can't think of a number within a second. That person must then move to the number 1 chair and everyone one else moves up a chair (the person in the first chair moves to chair number 2, person two moves to chair 3, and so forth). The person in chair number 1 now becomes the caller.

Play several rounds if time permits and youth are enjoying the game. Then **SAY,**

> **The Book of Revelation is full of numbers. We have already seen how the numbers can be symbolic of people, events, and ideas. Some of those ideas and events are in this next section of the book.**

Q&A
(20–30 minutes)

This is another chapter that could generate intense debate, depending upon information youth have picked up through popular culture. Remind youth of the focus: All the events in the Book of Revelation move toward the time when Satan, evil, and death will all be conquered, and all those who have lived faithful lives in Christlike love will dwell in the presence of God.

Have youth form three teams. Be sure each group has at least one Bible and a copy of *Unlocking the Mysteries*. Ask aloud any questions you choose from Chapter 4 or use the selected questions below. Award three points for the first team to get the correct answer. For added suspense make your final question worth twelve points. Refer to the FAQ indicated from *Unlocking the Mysteries* for the answers. Tally the points and congratulate the winners. Encourage discussion.

PRESS THE YOUTH TO GO DEEPER BY ALSO ASKING THESE QUESTIONS:

† **WHAT DO YOU THINK OF THESE ANSWERS?**

† **HOW DO THESE ANSWERS MAKE YOU FEEL?**

† What is the rapture? (FAQ 88, 89)

† What is the millennium? (FAQ 95)

† What is the great tribulation? (FAQ 90)

† What is Armageddon? (FAQ 87)

† What is the New Jerusalem? (FAQ 104)

† Where will the faithful spend eternity? (106)

† What is the lake of fire? (FAQ 98)

TIMELINE AND CREATIONS
(15–45 minutes)

Direct youth to the Revelation timeline and have them fill it in for Chapters 2, 7, 9, 13, 14, 16, 17, 19, 20, 21, and 22. Invite them to draw or write relevant material on the timeline.

Allow those who have begun other creative expressions (collages, montages, sculptures, paintings, songs, poems, skits, or journals) to continue work on their creations.

CLOSING
(Optional)

Close by reciting the greeting from Revelation 1:4:

> *Grace to you and peace from God who is and who was and who is to come...and from Jesus Christ.*

Send the group away with a theme song. (See introduction, page 7.)

Are These Sevens Lucky or Unlucky?

Focus:

The importance of the letters to the seven churches is to call Christians back to Jesus' view of faith: Faith should be lived out through action in the world.

Focus Scripture:

I know your works—your love, faith, service, and patient endurance. I know that your last works are greater than the first.

Revelation 2:19

Additional Scriptures:

Any of the Scriptures listed next to any of the FAQs in this section in *Unlocking the Mysteries.*

Materials:

✝ stuff for the Revelation timeline
✝ stuff for Revelation creations
✝ scrolls from Session 2
✝ copies of the "Lucky Sevens" chart
✝ one pair of dice (optional)

Before the Session:

Copy the "Lucky Sevens" chart. Gather materials and make sure you have everything prepared to continue the Revelation timeline and the activities you have chosen.

KEY POINTS

✝ The number 7 is often associated with perfection, closure, maturity, and completeness.

✝ The theme that unites the letters to the seven churches is reflected in two simple questions: "What are you doing with your life as a Christian?" and "Are you keeping the faith?" The letters carry the expectation that Christians need to live out their faith through acts of service and love.

✝ The plagues and destruction described in the cycles of seven seals, bowls, and trumpets symbolize God's judgment of evil and unfaithfulness. In the end all evil will be destroyed. These images provided hope to the Christians who were being persecuted.

BREAK THE SEAL
(10–15 minutes)

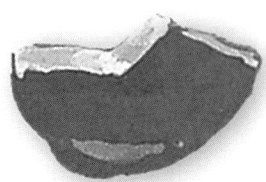

Now that your study is nearing its completion,
the time has come to see whose predictions
came true (see "Seal a Scroll," Session 2). If
your group is large, you will want to do this
activity in smaller teams. Gather the scrolls
from Session 2 and unseal them one at a time.
Read aloud the prediction and the name of the
predictor. Once the youth have had time to guess,

ASK:

Is (name of predictor) **a true prophet?**

Award prizes to the "true prophets." Then **SAY:**

**Remember that John the Revealer was a true prophet because he
spoke the words of God. As we will see in this next section, John's
message was that we are to live our faith in Jesus Christ through acts
of love and service.**

Q & A
(20–30 minutes)

This section contains a central message of the Book
of Revelation: Our faith should be lived out on a
daily basis through acts of love and service.
Although learning about the judgments unleashed
by the seven seals, bowls, and trumpets may be fascinating, the emphasis in this chapter should be placed on the message of
the letters to the seven churches.

Have youth divide into three teams. Be sure each group has at least one
Bible and a copy of *Unlocking the Mysteries.* Ask aloud any of the questions from Chapter 5, or use the selected questions below. Award three
points for the first team to get the correct answer. For added suspense
make your final question worth twelve points. Refer to the FAQ indicated
from *Unlocking the Mysteries* for the answers. Tally the points and congratulate the winners.

Encourage discussion.

† Why seven? (FAQ 108, 109, 110)

† What is important about the letters to the seven churches?
(FAQ 111)

† What is the common theme that unites these letters?
(FAQ 115)

† Why is the issue of faith and works so important to Revelation?
(FAQ 116)

PUSH YOUR YOUTH
TO GO DEEPER BY
ALSO ASKING THESE
QUESTIONS:

† **WHAT DO YOU
THINK OF THESE
ANSWERS?**

† **HOW DO THESE
ANSWERS MAKE
YOU FEEL?**

† What are the seven seals? (FAQ 133)

† What are the seven trumpets? (FAQ 134)

† What are the seven bowls? (FAQ 135)

 ## Key Question

What do these answers mean for how we live as Christians?

LUCKY SEVENS
(optional activity)

Show the group a pair of dice.

ASK:
   How many rolls will it take before I roll a seven?

Take guesses from various volunteers. Then roll the dice. Award a prize to the person who guessed correctly. Then **ASK:**

   What number is most common when rolling dice? Why?

Distribute copies of the "Lucky Sevens" chart (page 24) to show why seven is the easiest number to roll and therefore considered lucky.

TIMELINE AND CREATIONS
(15–45 minutes)

Direct youth to the Revelation timeline and have them fill it in for Chapters 2, 3, 5, 6, 8, 9, 10, 11, 15, and 16. Invite them to draw or write relevant material on the timeline.

Allow those who have begun Revelation creations (montages, collages, sculptures, paintings, songs, poems, skits, or journals) to continue work on their creations. Remind them that this is their last day to work on their projects. At the next session, they will present the projects to the group.

CLOSING
(Optional)

Close by reciting the greeting from Revelation 1:4:

   Grace to you and peace from God who is and who was and who is to come…and from Jesus Christ.

Send the group away with a theme song. (See introduction, page 7.)

LUCKY SEVENS

This chart demonstrates one reason why seven is considered a lucky number. When we roll two six-sided, numbered dice, there are more ways to roll combinations that add up to seven than any other number.

For example, imagine that you roll the dice and get a 3 and a 4. On the chart, locate a 3 on the top horizontal row and a 4 on the vertical row. By reading downward and finding where these rows intersect, you can see the sum of the numbers that you rolled.

FIRST DIE ROLLS...

	1	2	3	4	5	6
1	2	3	4	5	6	**7**
2	3	4	5	6	**7**	8
3	4	5	6	**7**	8	9
4	5	6	**7**	8	9	10
5	6	**7**	8	9	10	11
6	**7**	8	9	10	11	12

SECOND DIE ROLLS...

What Would Jesus Do,
AND WHAT WOULD JESUS HAVE US DO, ABOUT THE END OF THE WORLD?

Focus:
No one knows when the end of creation will come except God.

Focus Scripture:
But about that day and hour no one knows, neither the angels of heaven, nor the Son, but only the Father.

> Matthew 24:36

Additional Scriptures:
Matthew 24 and 25

Materials:
† stuff for the Revelation timeline
† stuff for Revelation creations
† two or three key padlocks with two keys each (You will need to save a key to make sure you will be able to open them even if the other keys are not found.)
† as many old, abandoned keys as you can find
† a box that can be locked as a "treasure chest"
† prizes for the treasure chest (prize possibilities include The Catacomb Project t-shirts, hats, and jewelry). See page 6 for additional information.

Before the Session:
Gather materials. Hide useless keys in or around your meeting area like you would hide eggs for an Easter egg hunt. Also hide the two or three real keys that unlock the treasure chest. Make sure you have everything prepared to complete the Revelation timeline. If necessary, make arrangements to present artistic creations.

KEY POINTS

When Jesus taught his disciples about the end of creation, he emphasized these things:

† Be careful about deception.

† Don't jump to conclusions about things that happen that are part of everyday life, because "the end is not yet."

† Focus on the eternal truths of my teachings; my word will never lose its value for your life.

† No one but God knows the day or hour when creation will come to a close.

KEY TO THE KINGDOM SEARCH
(10–15 minutes)

SAY:

> We have hidden keys all around the area. Some of the keys unlock the treasure chest filled with prizes. If you find one of those keys, you will share in the prize. You will have 10 minutes to search for the keys and to try them out on the treasure chest. Ready, Go!

Send the youth on the treasure hunt. If you feel creative, you could develop clues related to some of the imagery from the Revelation study.

 ## Q & A
(20–30 minutes)

Discussion about what Jesus taught about the end of creation is perhaps the most important one you will have as part of this study. It puts the problematic issues of Revelation into perspective.

Have youth form three teams. Be sure each group has at least one Bible and a copy of *Unlocking the Mysteries*. Ask aloud any of the questions from Chapter 6, or use the selected questions here. Award three points for the first team to get the correct answer. For added suspense make your final question worth twelve points. Refer to the FAQ indicated from *Unlocking the Mysteries* for the answers. Tally the points and congratulate the winners.

USE THESE QUESTIONS TO STIMULATE THE GROUP'S THINKING:

† **WHAT DO YOU THINK OF THESE ANSWERS?**

† **HOW DO THESE ANSWERS MAKE YOU FEEL?**

Invite further discussion.

† What does Jesus mean when he says, "The end is not yet"? (FAQ 142)

† Does Jesus know when the end will come? (FAQ 143)

† Does Jesus talk about the Second Coming? (FAQ 145)

† If we can't know for sure when the end of the world will occur, what should we do? (FAQ 146)

† What do Jesus' teachings and the Book of Revelation have in common? (FAQ 149)

† What is important about the Book of Revelation and Jesus' teachings about the end of the world? (FAQ 150)

Key Question

What do these answers mean for how we live as Christians?

TIMELINE AND CREATIONS

(30–60 minutes)

Direct youth to the Revelation timeline. Take time to review the chapters one by one. Ask participants to remember why they wrote or drew what they contributed for each chapter.

Allow those who have completed Revelation creations to present their creations.

You might want to plan a separate time for youth to present their creations to family, friends, and other church members.

CLOSING

Close by reciting the greeting from Revelation 1:4:

> *Grace to you and peace from God who is and who was and who is to come...and from Jesus Christ.*

Send the group away with a theme song. (See introduction, page 7.)

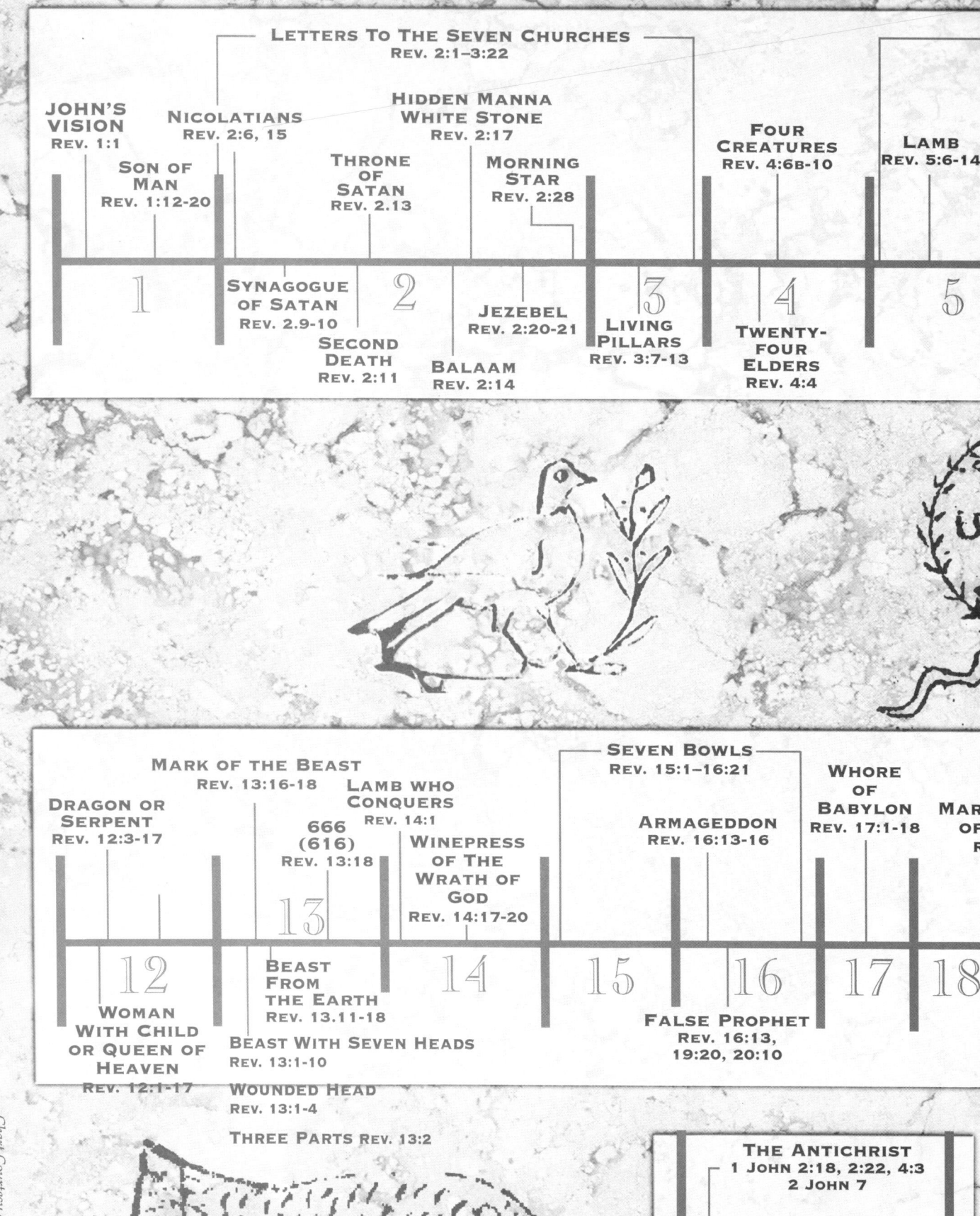

LETTERS TO THE SEVEN CHURCHES
REV. 2:1–3:22

JOHN'S VISION
REV. 1:1

NICOLAITANS
REV. 2:6, 15

HIDDEN MANNA
WHITE STONE
REV. 2:17

FOUR CREATURES
REV. 4:6B-10

LAMB
REV. 5:6-14

SON OF MAN
REV. 1:12-20

THRONE OF SATAN
REV. 2.13

MORNING STAR
REV. 2:28

1

SYNAGOGUE OF SATAN
REV. 2.9-10

2

JEZEBEL
REV. 2:20-21

3

4

5

SECOND DEATH
REV. 2:11

BALAAM
REV. 2:14

LIVING PILLARS
REV. 3:7-13

TWENTY-FOUR ELDERS
REV. 4:4

MARK OF THE BEAST
REV. 13:16-18

SEVEN BOWLS
REV. 15:1–16:21

WHORE OF BABYLON
REV. 17:1-18

MARK OF R

DRAGON OR SERPENT
REV. 12:3-17

LAMB WHO CONQUERS
REV. 14:1

666 (616)
REV. 13:18

WINEPRESS OF THE WRATH OF GOD
REV. 14:17-20

ARMAGEDDON
REV. 16:13-16

13

12

14

15

16

17

18

BEAST FROM THE EARTH
REV. 13.11-18

WOMAN WITH CHILD OR QUEEN OF HEAVEN
REV. 12:1-17

BEAST WITH SEVEN HEADS
REV. 13:1-10

FALSE PROPHET
REV. 16:13, 19:20, 20:10

WOUNDED HEAD
REV. 13:1-4

THREE PARTS REV. 13:2

THE ANTICHRIST
1 JOHN 2:18, 2:22, 4:3
2 JOHN 7

1 & 2 John

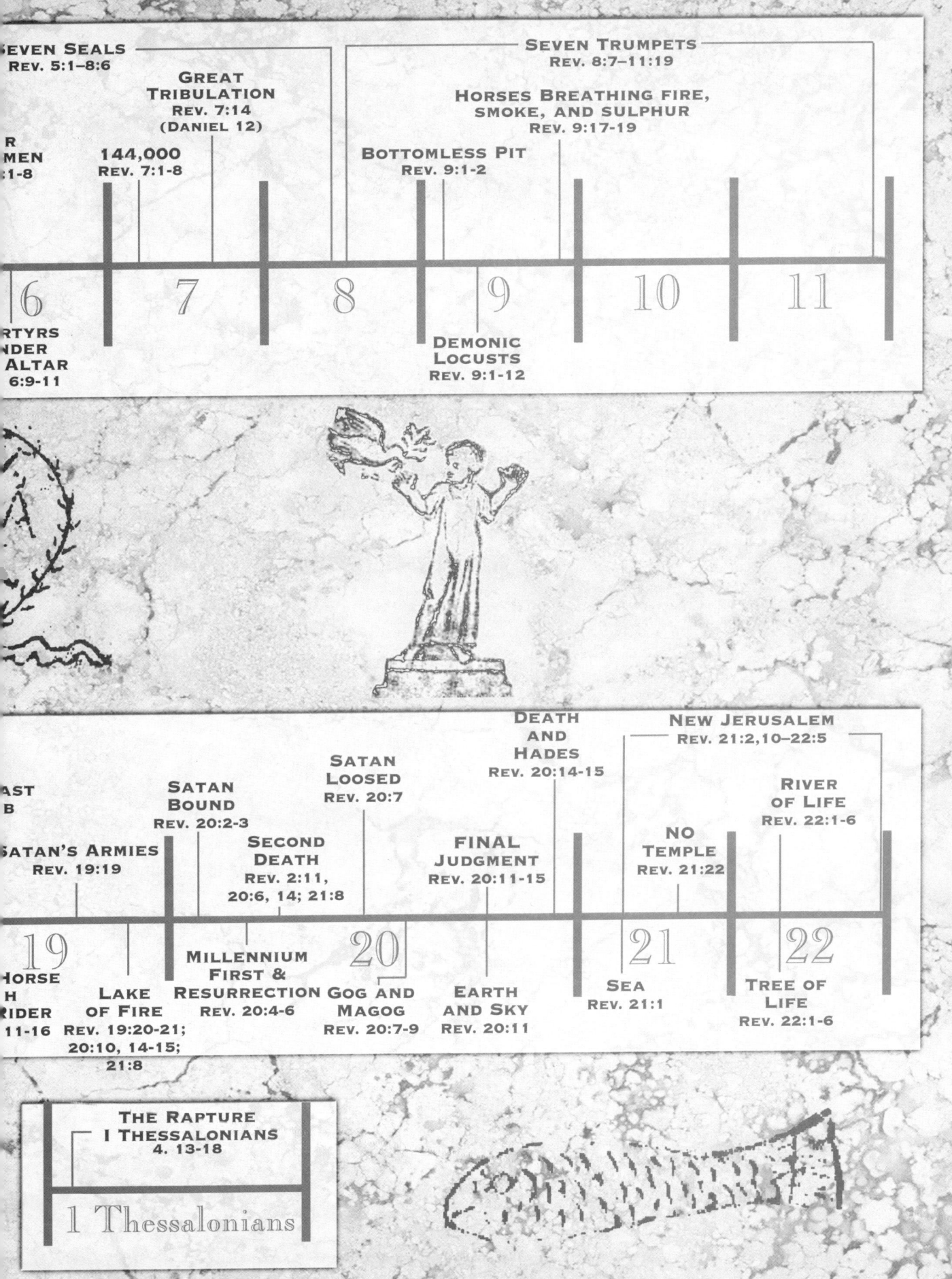

SEVEN SEALS
REV. 5:1–8:6

GREAT TRIBULATION
REV. 7:14
(DANIEL 12)

144,000
REV. 7:1-8

R
MEN
:1-8

RTYRS
NDER
ALTAR
6:9-11

6   7   8

SEVEN TRUMPETS
REV. 8:7–11:19

**HORSES BREATHING FIRE,
SMOKE, AND SULPHUR**
REV. 9:17-19

BOTTOMLESS PIT
REV. 9:1-2

**DEMONIC
LOCUSTS**
REV. 9:1-12

9   10   11

**DEATH
AND
HADES**
REV. 20:14-15

NEW JERUSALEM
REV. 21:2,10–22:5

**SATAN
LOOSED**
REV. 20:7

**SATAN
BOUND**
REV. 20:2-3

**RIVER
OF LIFE**
REV. 22:1-6

**NO
TEMPLE**
REV. 21:22

AST
B

Satan's Armies
REV. 19:19

**SECOND
DEATH**
REV. 2:11,
20:6, 14; 21:8

**FINAL
JUDGMENT**
REV. 20:11-15

19   20   21   22

HORSE
H
RIDER
11-16

**LAKE
OF FIRE**
REV. 19:20-21;
20:10, 14-15;
21:8

**MILLENNIUM
FIRST &
RESURRECTION**
REV. 20:4-6

**GOG AND
MAGOG**
REV. 20:7-9

**EARTH
AND SKY**
REV. 20:11

SEA
REV. 21:1

**TREE OF
LIFE**
REV. 22:1-6

**THE RAPTURE
I THESSALONIANS
4. 13-18**

1 Thessalonians

What Are the Catacombs?

After the death, resurrection, and ascension of Jesus Christ, the Christian message that "God is love" spread quickly throughout the world. The idea that anyone could be forgiven through grace and have eternal life had an immediate and irresistible appeal. The story of the resurrection and the presence of the living Christ in the world spoke to people's hearts and gave them confidence in life after death.

Anyone could be a Christian—slave or free, Jew or Greek, senator or gravedigger, man or woman. And, in the Christian community, everyone was considered equal in the eyes of God. The early Christians witnessed to their faith with great energy, conviction, and perseverance. They lived out the love they proclaimed through lives of service and acts of kindness.

At first the ruling Roman authorities were indifferent to this new belief and even found it somewhat intriguing. But when the Christians defied civil authority by refusing to worship the emperor and the pagan gods of Rome, the Roman authorities responded with hostility. Christians were accused of treason, sedition, insurrection, incest, ritual cannibalism, infanticide, and, ironically, atheism (because they refused to worship the emperor and the gods of Rome). In a superstitious world, they were blamed for natural disasters like fires, floods, plagues, and famines.

Prejudice and hatred toward the Christians grew quickly in the Roman Empire. At various times during the first and second centuries, Christians faced prison, torture, and even death for refusing to denounce Jesus Christ and worship the emperor. The persecutions of the first two centuries were not continuous or universal, and they were not always cruel and bloody. But they were always a threat lurking in the background of the Christian life. The catacombs were one of the places where the Christians sought refuge from these persecutions and felt free to express their Christian faith.

IN THE CATACOMBS, PERSECUTED CHRISTIANS FELT FREE TO EXPRESS THEIR FAITH.

FAQs About the Catacombs

WHAT ARE THE CATACOMBS?

Basically, the catacombs are underground cemeteries—tunnels lined with burial chambers that run for many miles under the cities of the ancient Roman Empire. They take the form of labyrinths of galleries and connecting chambers that are often arranged in layers as high as four stories, one above the other.

HOW WERE PEOPLE BURIED IN THE CATACOMBS?

The bodies were placed in niches hollowed out of the side walls of the tunnels, galleries, and chambers. Usually two or three bodies would be placed in a niche, which would be sealed off with stone slabs or large tiles.

WHY DID THE CHRISTIANS BURY THEIR DEAD IN THE CATACOMBS?

In the Roman Empire, open-air cemeteries above ground did exist, but the Christians chose to bury their dead underground for several reasons. It was difficult for Christians to own much land, and if they used the land for cemeteries, the space available would have been used up quickly. Because the early Christians rejected the idea of cremation in favor of being buried in a tomb as Christ was, they had to come up with a creative solution for burying all of the bodies of the dead in tombs. Most of the early Christians were poor, and it was cheaper to dig the winding underground system of tunnels, galleries, and chambers than to buy land above ground.

DID THE CHRISTIANS "INVENT" THE CATACOMBS?

No. This system of underground excavation was in place before Christianity, and it was not "caused" or "made necessary" by the persecutions in any way. The Christians simply took advantage of the engineering knowledge available to them at the time and developed it on a grand scale.

WHO DUG THE CATACOMBS?

The catacombs were dug by a special group of workers known as the *fossores* or gravediggers. They would dig for hours by the faint light of lamps, carrying out the dirt in baskets and bags. It took great skill and knowledge of excavation techniques to dig the tunnels and chambers in such a way that they would not collapse.

DID THE CHRISTIANS WORSHIP IN THE CATACOMBS?

Yes, but not all of the time. Because Roman law held that all places of burial were sacred, the catacombs were places of sanctuary. During the persecutions, Christians sometimes used the catacombs as a place of refuge where they could hold community meetings, celebrate Communion, and display their Christian symbols.

DID CHRISTIANS HIDE IN THE CATACOMBS DURING THE PERSECUTIONS?

No. The catacombs were never used as secret hiding places for Christians during times of persecutions. This idea is a myth created by movies and novels. Most Christians wanted to face the persecution as a way of witnessing to their faith. They only went into the catacombs to hold meetings, worship, and celebrate the Lord's Supper.

WHERE CAN I FIND MORE INFORMATION ABOUT CATACOMBS AND SEE WHAT THEY LOOK LIKE?

There are numerous websites that contain information and photographs of catacombs. Here are a few sites that you can explore:

http://www.catacombe.roma.it
http://www.iath.virginia.edu/mls4n/contents.html
http://www.kent.wednet.edu/curriculum/soc_studies/rome/Catacombs.html
http://myron.sjsu.edu/romeweb/CHRISTNS/christns.htm
http://www.encarta.msn.com/index/concise/0vol22/04262000.asp
http://www.csn.net/advent/cathen/03417b.htm

Catacomb Lock-In

Stepping Into the Catacomb

PREPARING FOR THE CATACOMB LOCK-IN

You should have a task force of youth counselors, cooperative parents, or adult volunteers prepared to "kidnap" or "smuggle" the youth to the catacomb where the main part of the retreat will take place. Let parents know well in advance that someone will be coming to pick up their children.

Make sure you copy, fill out, and have a parent sign the consent form on the back cover. You will want to make certain that you carefully explain to the parents what the youth will be doing at the lock-in. Also be sure to give them a list of what the youth will need for the retreat so that they will already be packed and ready to go. (This is especially important for friends of your youth group members who may be coming for the first time.)

The element of surprise is part of the fun of The Catacomb Project model. Depending on the number of youth who will be part of the event, you can use a church bus, a church van, or several family vans assigned to pick up the youth and transport them to the retreat site. If you use several family cars and vans, you may wish to caravan in order to keep the youth together and let them participate in the rest of the "kidnappings." If the youth will be picked up by several people or in several trips, be sure to have something prepared for them to do while they are waiting. (Snacks or games usually work well.)

CREATING THE CATACOMB

Pick out a room in the church that is large enough for your youth group to be comfortable. If the church doesn't have adequate space, consider using an area of a local school, the church parsonage, a youth's or youth leader's home. During this experience you will work together as a large group, but you also will need to break into smaller teams for discussion purposes. If you wish, make provision for the youth group to eat together and sleep in that same room.

Cover any windows and turn down the air a bit to ensure that the room is cool and dark to simulate the cool, damp atmosphere of an underground cave. Provide only dim light, or preferably, light the room with candles. (Be sure to take all necessary precautions to use candles safely.) You can decorate the room as elaborately as you wish to give it the look and feel of an underground burial chamber in the catacombs. Line the walls with cardboard and draw or paint depictions of the tombs stacked one upon the other up to the ceiling. If you wish, you can save this task until after the youth arrive and you have described to them what is taking place. They can also decorate the walls with the Christians symbols found in the catacombs.

OPTIONAL: ONE WAY

We have included instructions for one way to decorate your retreat space. Remember: Your catacomb can be as elaborate or as simple as you choose. The only requirements are for you to use your imagination and creativity, and for you and your group to have fun!

In order to create an attractive, eerie entrance to your catacombs, follow the directions below. Be sure to work in a well-ventilated area. Note that you will need several hours of drying time between steps (see *).

Materials

These supplies are available at a home repair store, such as Home Depot or Lowes, and cost less than $100.00.

† Six 4-by-eight-foot $\frac{3}{4}$-inch Styrofoam® boards—the kind used for building insulation
† Two tubes adhesive—the kind that comes in a caulking gun tube (Liquid Nails® is one brand.)
† $\frac{1}{2}$ gallon dark brown latex paint
† 1 quart light brown latex paint
† 1 quart cream-colored latex paint
   (For inexpensive paint, ask for samples from the mistakenly mixed section.)
† Two cans spray foam insulation
† 1 quart acetone
† wooden paint brushes with natural bristles (important for applying the acetone)
† foam paint brushes (for applying paint only)
† paint roller (optional)
† duct tape
† knife or screwdriver

Directions:

1. Peel the plastic coating off the foam board. Use adhesive to attach two panels back to back. Do the same with the other two sets of panels so that you have three panels that are each $1\frac{1}{2}$ inches thick. Place bricks, books, or other heavy objects on the corners of the panels while they dry. *Let dry for at least four hours.

2. On one panel, draw and cut out a doorway. (See illustration.)

3. Paint one side of the panels with dark brown paint, using a roller or foam brushes. *Let the paint dry. (Latex paint dries fairly fast, depending on how thick is it applied.)

4. Draw a rock pattern on the panels. (See illustration.) Allow about one inch around rocks to simulate mortar.

5. Score (cut) around rocks in the center of the one-inch mortar. Cut about $\frac{1}{2}$ -inch deep. (This will allow the acetone to do its work.)

6. Using the small wooden, natural-bristled brushes, apply acetone to the scored areas. The acetone will eat away the foam board wherever it is applied, delineating the rocks and simulating the mortar around the rocks.

7. Apply spray foam to some rocks to add texture and dimension. *Let dry for at least four hours. (Different brands have different drying times.)

8. Paint the crevices and textured rocks with dark brown paint. After the paint dries, apply the lighter colors with the tip of a paint brush, using a stippling motion, for finishing touches.

9. Use duct tape to attach the three panels at the back. You can stand them as pictured or straighten them into a wall.

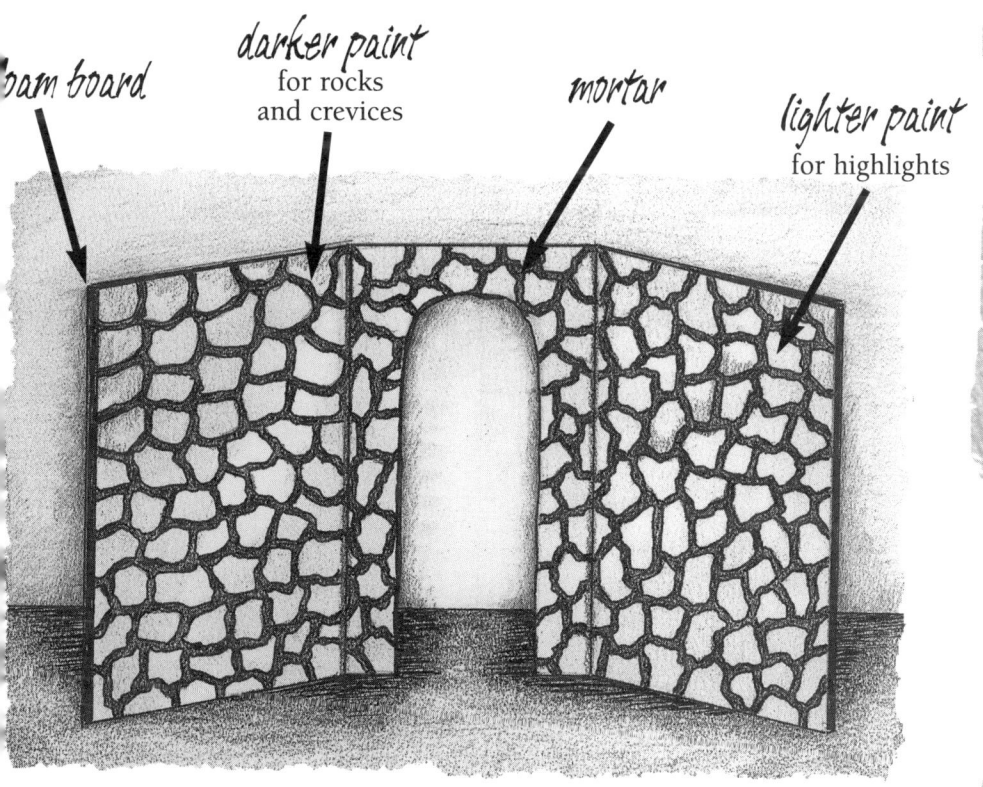

foam board

darker paint
for rocks
and crevices

mortar

lighter paint
for highlights

Catacomb Session 1:
RECONSTRUCTING THE CHRISTIAN FAITH

Materials:
† several large pads of paper
† markers
† at least two copies of FAQs about the Catacombs (pages 31–32)

IN THE CATACOMBS
(20–30 minutes)

After the youth have had some time to settle in and get focused, gather the group and say something like:

> You have been kidnapped and brought to this place because it is now against the law to be a Christian. If you profess your faith publicly, you could be humiliated, separated from your family, placed in prison, tortured, or even put to death. You are living like the early Christians who worshipped in the catacombs.

If you have decorated the room like a catacomb, invite the youth to talk about what they see and about what they already know about catacombs. Some youth may have studied the subject at school.

Have a volunteer read aloud the Catacombs FAQs (pages 31–32). Have another volunteer read the answers. Encourage the youth to ask their own questions about the catacomb setting.

If you have not decorated the room, now is a good time to involve the youth in creating the catacomb atmosphere. See page 34 for suggestions.

REMEMBER THE BIBLE
(45–60 minutes)

After a short break, say to the group:

> We are no longer allowed to possess anything that is part of the Christian faith. You may not have Bibles, hymnals, or Christian books or magazines. All Christian material has been confiscated by the authorities.

> Our first task is to reconstruct the Christian faith from what we know and remember about the Bible. You don't have a printed copy of the Bible to rely on, so you need to remember as many of the Bible verses and stories as you can.

Have youth work in teams of five or six, and give each team a pad of paper and a marker. Ask them to try to remember whatever they can in response to the following questions and to write the answers on their pads:

† **What ideas do you remember from the Bible?**

† **What Scriptures have you memorized?**

† **What stories do you remember?**

As the teams fill sheets of paper with Scripture information, post them on the walls.

Bring the group back together and have teams explain what they have written on their pads. Talking about what they have written will help them remember more. Encourage this dialogue.

Then ask the group to identify what the basic and necessary beliefs of Christianity are. Have someone write the group's answers on a large sheet of paper.

As the lock-in progresses, continue to encourage youth to add to the lists.

Catacomb Session 2:
BEING CHRISTIAN WHEN
IT IS HARD TO BE A CHRISTIAN

Materials:
† several large pads of paper
† markers.
† copies of the quotations on pages 46–47

ANCIENT PERSECUTION
(20 minutes)

Divide into teams again. Give each team one or more of the quotations copied from pages 46–47. You can download additional quotations on the World Wide Web at (www.catacombproject.com).

Tell the teams that these quotations are observations by various writers from the time of the first persecutions of Christians. Ask the team to talk about each of the quotations and then write their answers to the following questions on a sheet of paper:

† What does this statement say about what it means to be a Christian?

† What does this statement say about how we should live our lives?

WHAT WAS IT LIKE?
(30 minutes)

Bring the group back together. You may wish to hand out additional copies of the quotations to members of the other teams for this discussion. Have each team tell what they learned about the way Christians lived and were perceived during the persecutions of the first and second centuries. Guide them with the following questions. Encourage discussion.

† What were the persecutions like for the Christians of the first and second centuries?

† How did these Christians live?

† How did the world see them?

† Do we have the same qualities in our Christian walk today that they had back then? Refer the youth to their team's sheets of paper from the previous activity.

PSALMS, HYMNS, SPIRITUAL SONGS
(20–60 minutes)

After a break, SAY:

One way Christians have continued to find strength even in persecution is through music—psalms, hymns, gospel music, Christian music, and spirituals.

Have the group work together to remember hymns or Christian songs that can sustain them. Have a volunteer begin either by singing or by calling out the name of a song. Have the entire group sing along. If you want, have someone write the titles or the entire songs on a sheet of paper as you sing. If your group is not comfortable singing in this manner, invite them to call out titles and words to be written.

Allow time for youth to add to the Bible, belief, and music lists.

Catacomb Session 3:
THE PERSECUTION OF CHRISTIANS TODAY

Materials:
† several large pads of paper
† markers
† copies of the quotations on page 48
† copies of the symbols from page 45; cut the page into strips, each with
   a symbol and its write-up.

Optional:
One or more computers with Internet access. If you are not able to have
the equipment for use during the lock-in, check with some of your youth
in advance. They may be able to visit the websites from their home computers and bring in the print-outs to the group at the lock-in.

PRESENT PERSECUTION
(20 minutes)

Divide into teams again. Give each of the teams copies of one or more of
the quotations on page 48. Additional information is available on the
World Wide Web at (www.catacombproject.com) or from the other sites
listed at the end of this section.

Have the teams answer these questions on their pad of paper:

† **What does this quotation say about what it means to be a
   Christian?**

† **What does this quotation say how we should live our lives?**

(For more detailed descriptions of the present-day persecution of
Christians worldwide, refer to Nina Shea's *In the Lion's Den: A Shocking
Account of Persecution and Martyrdom of Christians Today and How We
Should Respond*, ISBN 0-8054-6357-7.)

GO ONLINE
(Optional)

As an optional activity, allow the small groups to find out more about the
persecuted church through links from The Catacomb Project website
(www.catacombproject.com). These sites provide up-to-the-minute information on the present-day persecution of Christians worldwide. Encourage
youth to take notes and print interesting information. Discuss the findings.
Here is a list of possible sites to visit:

Voice of the Martyrs: http://www.persecution.com
International Christian Concern: http://www.persecution.org
Amnesty International: http://www.amnesty.org
Ethics and Religious Liberty Commission: http://www.erlc.com

WHAT IS IT LIKE?
(30–45 minutes)

Bring the group back together and have each team tell what they learned about the persecution of Christians in our own time. Guide them with the following questions:

† Did it shock you to learn about the present-day persecution of Christians worldwide?

† How do these Christians set an example for us?

† How do you think you would respond to persecution?

† Have you ever felt "persecuted" for what you believe? What fears do you have about expressing your faith? being rejected? ostracized? bullied? disrespected? or worse?

† When is it difficult for you to stand up as a Christian?

† What are the consequences for you?

† Would you be a Christian if it meant humiliation, segregation, prison, torture, or even death?

BELIEFS AND PRACTICES
(20–30 minutes)

After a break, gather the group together and SAY,

Christians are identified by what they believe and what they practice.

ASK:
† Can you think of any statements of belief that we haven't already mentioned?

† What do Christians do that makes us Christian?

Have a volunteer add these beliefs and practices to the sheet of paper. If the youth do not identify these, remind them of traditional creeds and of practices such as baptism and the Lord's Supper.

SYMBOLS
(10–20 minutes)

SAY something like:
The last things to add to our papered walls are symbols of our faith in Jesus Christ.

Ask for pairs of volunteers. Give each pair a symbol and its description (page 45). Have one partner read about the symbol while the other partner draws it on a sheet of paper.

Catacomb Session 4:
A Worship Service

Materials:

✝ 41 candles plus one candle for each youth; choose candles of different shapes, colors, and sizes.
✝ face paints or finger paints
✝ clergy person to celebrate the Lord's Supper
✝ Communion elements

What Sustains Us?
(10–15 minutes)

Draw everyone together again. Ask for them to get comfortable, close their eyes, and listen as you take them on a guided meditation. Read the following slowly, pausing to allow the listeners to fill in with their own imaginations:

> You finally feel safe here in the catacomb. As you wait for the others to come, you think about the blame, the threats, the fear you experience outside this place. But here, things are different. You look around in the dim light. On the walls your friends have written reminders of what Jesus said. There are drawings too. You smile to yourself. Those same drawings are outside too, but the persecutors don't know what they mean—just you and the others who will gather here. A song comes to mind. You hear it and recall times of singing as people come forward for the Lord's Supper. In these holy moments, with your Christian friends, you renew your courage. You know you must leave this safe place, but you know in your heart that God is with you.

Give the youth a few moments to reenter from their journey. Then ask these questions:

✝ **How does God sustain people during hard times?**

✝ **How do you experience God when you are struggling?**

If your group has already studied the Book of Revelation, you may wish to bring into the discussion the role of that book in giving people hope and courage (if the youth do not).

Creating the Worship Service
(30–45 minutes)

Have the youth design a worship service based on what they have learned during this experience. The youth should be responsible for the entire

service. Let them use the Bible verses, creeds, songs, and professions of faith posted around the room as the foundation of the service. They may include the following elements in the service:

- Prayers for the Persecuted
- Christian Symbol Face Painting
- The Lord's Supper
- Personal Candles

You may wish to make copies of the instructions below to give to the youth. Depending upon the time and the number of youth, you may want to assign teams to prepare the various parts.

PRAYERS FOR THE PERSECUTED

Prayers for the persecuted should be a part of the worship service. These prayers should include thanksgiving for the witness of the Christians who suffered the persecutions of the first and second centuries as well as prayers for present-day Christians who are persecuted.

The Voice of the Martyrs (www.persecution.com) offers the following guidelines for praying for the persecuted. Since neither the youth leader nor the youth have access to a Bible during this retreat, use the following Scriptures to guide your prayers for those who are persecuted.

1. Pray for those in prison that they would know they are not forgotten: "Remember the prisoners as if chained with them—those who are mistreated—since you yourselves are in the body also" (Hebrews 13:3).

2. Pray that the needs of the families of those who have been martyred would be met abundantly: "Now to him who is able to do exceedingly abundantly above all that we can ask or think, according to the power that works in us" (Ephesians 3:20).

3. Pray that the government and prison officials in countries where Christians are persecuted would be drawn into a relationship with Christ: "No one can come to me unless the Father who sent me draws him; and I will raise him up at the last day" (John 6:44).

4. Pray that Christians would love those who are persecuting them: "But I say to you, love your enemies, bless those who curse you, do good to those who hate you, and pray for those who spitefully use you and persecute you" (Matthew 5:44).

5. Pray that God would give new ways to get Bibles and other forms of help to Christians in restricted nations: "Meanwhile praying also for us, that God would open to us a door for the word, to speak the mystery of Christ, for which I am also in chains" (Colossians 4:3).

Scripture quotations from The New King James Version. Copyright © 1979, 1980, 1982, Thomas Nelson Inc., Publishers. Prayers are used by permission of The Voice of the Martyrs

On page 44 is a list of countries where there is known persecution or severe discrimination against Christians. Set up forty-one candles on a table or altar and have the youth take turns lighting a candle for Christians being persecuted in each of these nations. Ask the youth to say a prayer of their own or the one below as each of the candles is lit:

We light this candle to symbolize the Christians who are presently living under persecution in (insert country). **We pray that one day they will be able to proclaim the name of Jesus Christ in freedom and peace.**

CHRISTIAN SYMBOL FACE PAINTING

As a passing of the peace, have the youth pair off, choose a Christian symbol for their partner, and paint it on each other's forehead or cheek to symbolize that they belong to Jesus Christ.

Painters may use fingers or thin brushes. Be sure to have paper towels readily available for clean up. If you feel the youth will not be comfortable with face painting, they could paint more symbols on the sheets of paper lining the walls.

THE LORD'S SUPPER

Invite your pastor to celebrate the Lord's Supper. As part of their reconstructing the practices of the faith from memory, the youth may have recalled some of the liturgy of Holy Communion. If the pastor is willing, have him or her use what the youth remembered as a foundation for their Communion service on this day.

PERSONAL CANDLES

Close worship with a moment of personal commitment. Have each person choose a candle from among the different sizes, shapes, and colors. As each person lights a candle, have him or her place it on the altar, saying something like:

This candle symbolizes my witness to the love of God in my life. I am thankful for the freedom to proclaim Jesus Christ is Lord!

The following is a list of countries where there is known persecution or severe discrimination against Christians.

Algeria	Libya
Azerbaijan	Macedonia
Bangladesh	Mexico
Bhutan	Morocco
Burma	Nepal
China	Nigeria
Columbia	North Korea
Cuba	Pakistan
Egypt	Peru
Ethiopia	Philippines
Germany	Romania
Haiti	Russia
India	Rwanda
Indonesia	Saudi Arabia
Iran	Sri Lanka
Israel	Sudan
Jordan	Turkey
Kazakhstan	Vietnam
Kuwait	Uzbekistan
Laos	Yemen
Latvia	

CHRISTIAN SYMBOLS FROM THE CATACOMBS

Early Christians painted and carved symbols in the catacombs as visible reminders of their faith. For the Christians of the first and second centuries these symbols embodied the meaning of gospel and the peace of eternal life in the presence of God.

To symbolize Jesus Christ and those Christ has saved, early Christians depicted The Good Shepherd with a lamb around his shoulders.

The fish is common today as the Greek acrostic IXTHYS (*ichtùs*). The letters stand for the first letters in the phrase: *Iesùs Christòs Theòu Uiòs Sotèr* = Jesus Christ, Son of God, Saviour.

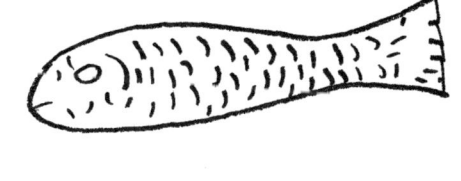

The figure praying with open arms, the *orante*, symbolizes the soul living in divine peace.

The dove holding an olive branch was a symbol of peace for the early Christians much as it is for us today.

The *Chi Rho* is the monogram of Christ, formed by interlacing two letters of the Greek alphabet: *X* (*chi*) and *P* (*rho*), which are the first two letters of the Greek word *Christòs* or Christ.

This symbol consists of the *Chi Rho*, the monogram for Christ, placed between the *Alpha* and *Omega*, the first and the last letters of the Greek alphabet. This symbol signifies that Christ is the beginning and the end of all things.

The anchor symbolizes the hope of Christian salvation.

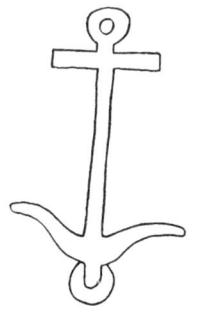

REVELATION: UNLOCKING THE MYSTERIES WITH YOUTH

Early Persecution

I. Christians are not different because of their country or the language they speak or the way they dress. They do not isolate themselves in their cities nor use a private language; even the life they lead has nothing strange. Their doctrine does not originate from the elaborate disquisitions of intellectuals, nor do they follow, as many do, philosophical systems which are the fruit of human thinking. They live in Greek or in barbarian cities, as the case may be, and adapt themselves to local traditions in dress, food and all usage. Yet they testify to a way which, in the opinion of the many, has something extraordinary about it.

From the "Letter to Diognetus" (by an unknown author of the Second Century).

II. They obey the laws of the state, but in their lives they go beyond the law. They love everyone, yet are persecuted by everyone. No one really knows them, but all condemn them. They are killed, but go on living. They are poor, but enrich many. They have nothing, but abound in everything. But in that contempt they find glory before God. Their honour is insulted, while their justice is acknowledged.

From the "Letter to Diognetus" (by an unknown author of the Second Century).

III. They strictly observe the commandments of the Lord, by living in a saintly and right way, as the Lord God has prescribed to them; they give Him thanks each morning and evening for all food and drink and every other thing. These are, O Emperor, their laws; the goods they have to ask God, they ask Him, and so they pass through this world till the end of time; because God has subjected everything to them. Therefore they are grateful to Him, because the whole universe and all creation have been made for them. Surely these people have found truth.

From the "Apology" by Aristides (Second Century)

REVELATION: UNLOCKING THE MYSTERIES WITH YOUTH

IV. They help those who offend them, making friends of them; do good to their enemies. They don't adore idols; they are kind, good, modest, sincere, they love one another; don't despise widows; protect the orphans; those who have much give without grumbling, to those in need. When they meet strangers, they invite them to their homes with joy, for they recognize them as true brothers, not natural but spiritual.

From the "Apology" by Aristides (Second Century)

V. I shall pay homage to the emperor, but will not adore him; I shall instead pray for him. I adore the true and only God, by whom I know the sovereign was made. Well now, you might ask me: "Why don't you adore the emperor?" The emperor, given authority by God, must be honoured with a proper respect, but he must not be adored. You see, he is not God; he is only a man whom God has placed in that office not to be adored, but in order that he exercise justice on earth. In a way this authority was entrusted to him by God. As the emperor may not tolerate that his title be taken over by those subject to him, so no one may be adored, save God. The sovereign must therefore be honoured with sentiments of reverence; we must obey him and pray for him: In this way God's will is done.

From the "Books to Autolicus" of S. Theophilus of Antioch (Second Century)

Persecution Today

"More Christians have died for their faith in the 20th Century than in the previous 19 centuries combined. More than any other faith, Christians around the world are suffering brutal persecution....The examples are heartbreakingly plentiful. The list of afflictions reads like an alphabet of cruelty: amputation, bombing, crucifixion, displacement, flogging, kidnapping, murder, prison, rape, slavery, and torture. The sheer dimensions of the problem are mind-boggling."

"In Sudan, the Muslim government has made it a crime to convert to Christianity—a policy enforced brutally. As the Khartoum government troops move south, where most Christians live, believers are given three options: convert, flee, or be killed."

"In Vietnam Christians are subject to arrest, threats, and confiscation of their homes."

"In North Korea Christians are forced to meet secretly in private homes, and they have no access to Bibles or religious materials."

"In Iran four prominent evangelical pastors have been abducted and assassinated in the last few years."

"Police in Saudi Arabia have arrested and abused hundreds of Christians—believers whose only crime was engaging in religious activities. Citizens are paid a bounty of three thousand dollars for exposing a home Bible study class."

"In China up to 100 million Christians risk their lives daily by defying government orders banning free worship."

From *In the Lion's Den: A Shocking Account of Persecution and Martyrdom of Christians Today and How We Should Respond* by Nina Shea; Copyright © 1997 by Broadman Holman Press. Used by permission.

REVELATION: UNLOCKING THE MYSTERIES WITH YOUTH